You Got This!

A motivational guide for
achieving your goals.

You Got This!

A motivational guide for achieving your goals.

by
James Kademan

Business Coach with
Draw In Customers Business Coaching

Copyright © 2017

Draw In Customers Business Coaching presents, You Got This!, A
Motivational Guide for Achieving Your Goals.
Written by James Kademan.

Copyright 2017

Thank you for purchasing this book. By using the information and advice
given within, you will advance your career, achieve your dreams and make it
to the tippy top of whatever mountain you want to climb. Do so at your own
risk. Draw In Customers, James Kademan, and everybody else that is not
you is not responsible for your actions. You are.

Visit **www.drawincustomers.com** for more information about succeeding in
life and business. Now get to reading. You got this!

ISBN: 978-0-9990258-0-2 softcover
ISBN: 978-0-9990258-1-9 ebook

Check out the last printed page. That's the important part.

You Got This!

You Got This!

You Got This!

You

Got

This!

You Got This!

You Got This!

You Got This!

You Got This!

You Got This!

You Got This!

You Got This!

You
Got
This!

You Got This!

You Got This!

You Got This!

You Got This!

You Got This!

You Got This!

You Got This!

You Got This!

You Got This!

You Got This!

You Got This!

You Got This!

You Got This!

You Got This!

You Got This!

You Got This!

You Got This!

You Got This!

You Got This!

You Got This!

You Got This!

You

Got

This!

You Got This!

You Got This!

You Got This!

You Got This!

You Got This!

You Got This!

You
Got
This!

You Got This!

You Got This!

You
Got
This!

You Got This!

You Got This!

You Got This!

You Got This!

You Got This!

You Got This!

You Got This!

You Got This!

You Got This!

You Got This!

You Got This!

You Got This!

You

Got

This!

You Got This!

You
Got
This!

You Got This!

You Got This!

You Got This!

You Got This!

You Got This!

You Got This!

You Got This!

You Got This!

You Got This!

You Got This!

You Got This!

You

Got

This!

You

Got

This!

You
Got
This!

You Got This!

You

Got

This!

You Got This!

You Got This!

You

Got

This!

You Got This!

You

Got

This!

You Got This!

You

Got

This!

You

Got

This!

You Got This!

You Got This!

You

Got

This!

You Got This!

You Got This!

You Got This!

You Got This!

You Got This!

You Got This!

You Got This!

You Got This!

You Got This!

You Got This!

You Got This!

You
Got
This!

You Got This!

You Got This!

You Got This!

You
Got
This!

You Got This!

You Got This!

You Got This!

You Got This!

You

Got

This!

You Got This!

You Got This!

You Got This!

You Got This!

You Got This!

You

Got

This!

You Got This!

You Got This!

You Got This!

You Got This!

You Got This!

You Got This!

You Got This!

You
Got
This!

You Got This!

You

Got

This!

You Got This!

You Got This!

You Got This!

You Got This!

You Got This!

You Got This!

You Got This!

You Got This!

You Got This!

You Got This!

You Got This!

You Got This!

You Got This!

You

Got

This!

You
Got
This!

You Got This!

You Got This!

You Got This!

You Got This!

You Got This!

You
Got
This!

You Got This!

You Got This!

You
Got
This!

You Got This!

You Got This!

You

Got

This!

You Got This!

You
Got
This!

You Got This!

You Got This!

You Got This!

You Got This!

You Got This!

You Got This!

You
Got
This!

You Got This!

You Got This!

You Got This!

You

Got

This!

You Got This!

You Got This!

You
Got
This!

You Got This!

You Got This!

You Got This!

You Got This!

You Got This!

You Got This!

You Got This!

You Got This!

You

Got

This!

You Got This!

You Got This!

You
Got
This!

You Got This!

You Got This!

You

Got

This!

You
Got
This!

You

Got

This!

You

Got

This!

You Got This!

You Got This!

You Got This!

You Got This!

You Got This!

You Got This!

You Got This!

You
Got
This!

You Got This!

You Got This!

You

Got

This!

You

Got

This!

You Got This!

You Got This!

You

Got

This!

You Got This!

You Got This!

You Got This!

You
Got
This!

You
Got
This!

You Got This!

You Got This!

You Got This!

You Got This!

You Got This!

You Got This!

You

Got

This!

You Got This!

You Got This!

You
Got
This!

You Got This!

You Got This!

You Got This!

You Got This!

You Got This!

You
Got
This!

You Got This!

You
Got
This!

You
Got
This!

You Got This!

You

Got

This!

You Got This!

You Got This!

You
Got
This!

You Got This!

You Got This!

You

Got

This!

You Got This!

You
Got
This!

You Got This!

You
Got
This!

You Got This!

You
Got
This!

You

Got

This!

You Got This!

You Got This!

You Got This!

You Got This!

You Got This!

You Got This!

You Got This!

Now get to work.

Now get to work.

www.ingramcontent.com/pod-product-compliance
Lightning Source LLC
Chambersburg PA
CBHW070600300426
44113CB00010B/1343